I LOVE DRESSAGE

Coloring Book

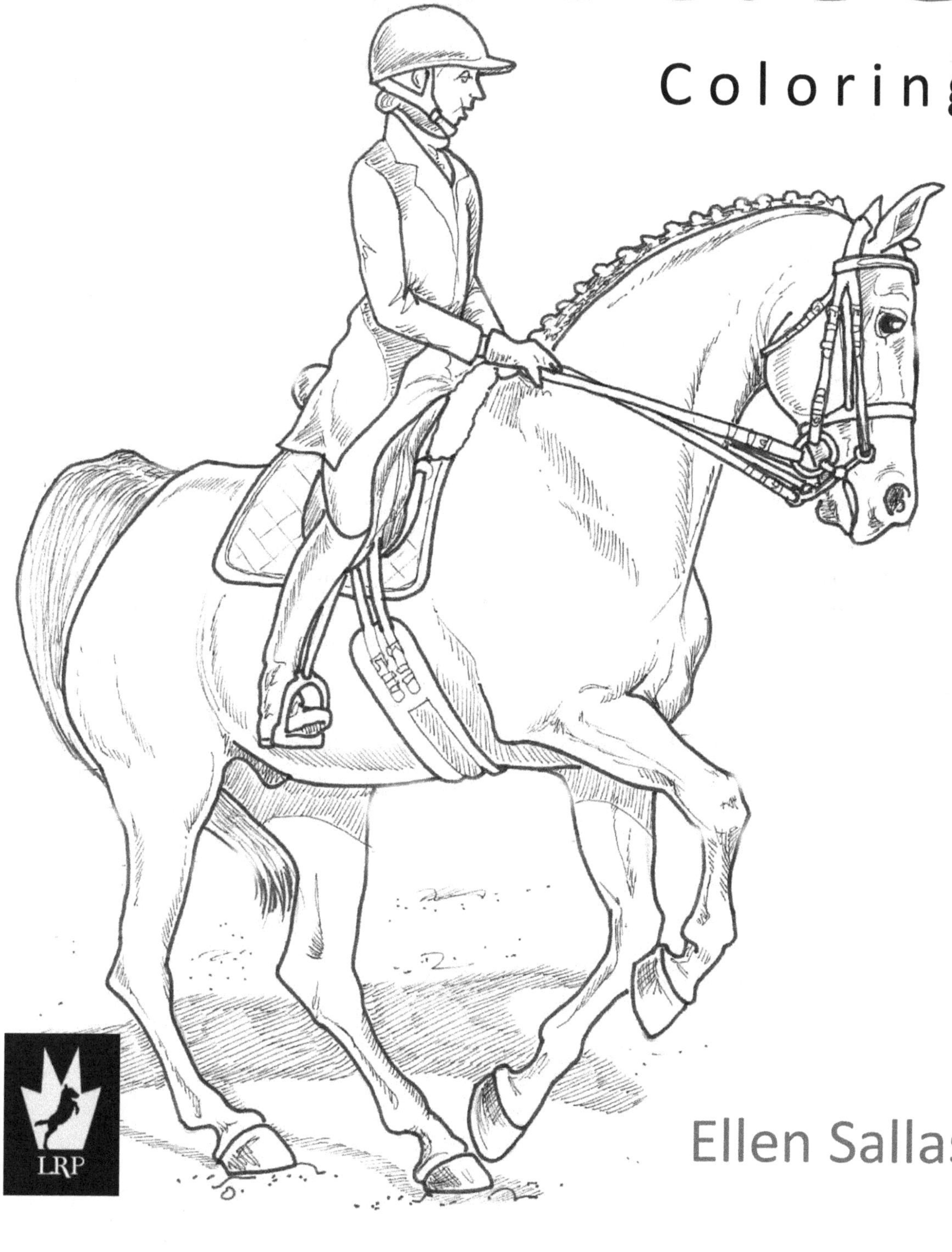

Ellen Sallas

I Love Dressage Coloring Book
All Rights Reserved
Copyright © 2016 Ellen Sallas

Updated 2-19-2024

ISBN-13: 978-0692653197
ISBN-10: 0692653198

Little Roni Publishers / Byhalia, MS
www.littleronipublishers.com
@LittleRoniPublishers

This book may not be reproduced, transmitted, or stored in whole or in part by any means, including graphic, electronic, or mechanical without the express written consent of the publisher except in the case of brief quotations embodied in critical articles and reviews.

Written and illustrated by Ellen Sallas, a.k.a Ellen C. Maze

PUBLISHED IN THE UNITED STATES OF AMERICA

Dressage is an equestrian sport defined by the International Equestrian Federation as "the highest expression of horse training." *Dressage* is a French word which means "training."

The discipline has ancient roots in the writings of Xenophon, a Greek historian student of Socrates (430-354 BC) who mastered horse training for the purpose of use in war.

All horses can benefit from the basic riding principles of dressage, but at the upper levels, dressage horses are specifically bred for the sport. Warmblood breeds are the most common at international FEI competitions.

Arabian horses often excel in dressage, even at the top levels. Look for Polish lines, which provide consistent size and bone, as well as temperament.

When asked about Fjords, Dressage Olympian Lendon Gray was quoted saying, "They're not dressage horses, but every barn should have one." It is fascinating to discover that the unflappable and intelligent Fjord is seen often at Grand Prix level, and winning!

The Freisian is a carriage horse; its natural conformation often prevents the "throughness" required at the upper levels. Still, they are amiable, athletic, and willing, and many can be seen up to Fourth Level.

In 1994, the USEF passed a rule to permit mules to compete in dressage; a few stars have competed and won at Fourth Level. Mule enthusiasts assert mules are harder to train than horses, but they are smarter and can be more loyal than any horse breed.

Spooks and shies are quite common at any level of competition. Riders will do their best to expose their mounts to flags, flowers, and other odd things, but going to shows often is the best way to desensitize a wide-eyed dressage mount.

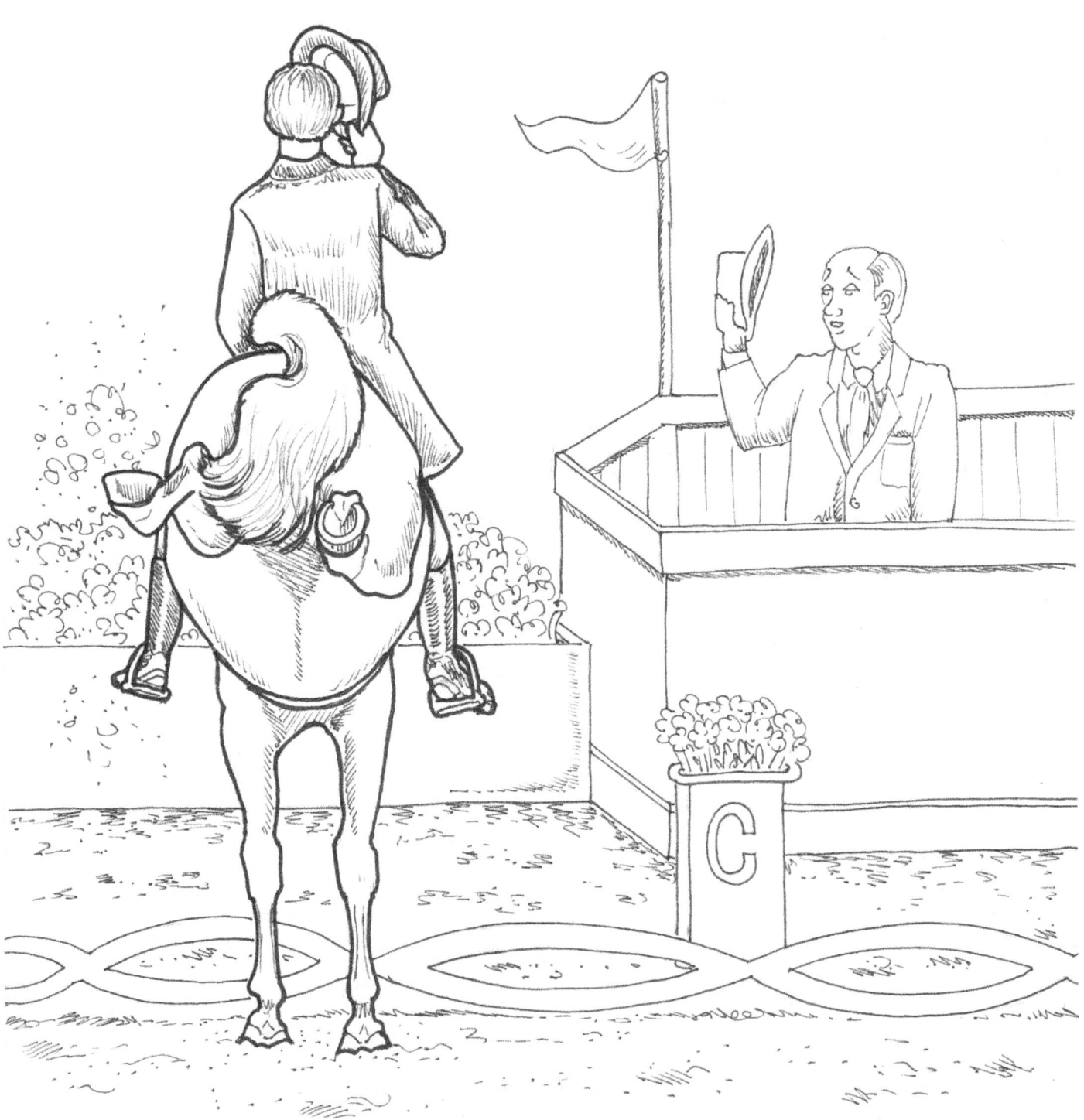

Riders don't always see what has spooked their horse. The horse is a prey animal, so it has a strong instinct to flee perceived danger. Consistent training will help you stay in the saddle and whisper calming words to your spooked mount.

Sometimes a horse will spook or shy because of undiagnosed discomfort. Always have a vet check the horse for back, hoof, or tooth pain – some common culprits when a normally quiet horse bolts under saddle.

This is Olympian Michael Poulin with champion dressage master Graf George, a Hanoverian, (1982-2008).

Enter the arena, halt square, and salute. Execute the salute by putting both reins in your left hand, lowering your straightened right arm next to your leg and nodding at the judge. Once the judge nods back pick up both reins and begin the test.

In the extended trot, the horse lengthens its stride to the maximum length through great forward thrust and reach.

In the pirouette, the horse makes a 360° circle with its front end around a smaller circle made by the hind end, all the while, the horse remains slightly bent in the direction of travel.

The piaffe is a calm, composed, elevated trot in place. The center of gravity of the horse is more towards the hind end, with the hindquarters slightly lowered with great bending of the joints in the hind legs. The front end of the horse remains light.

The piaffe was originally used in battle to keep the horse focused, warm, and moving, ready to surge forward into battle. In modern times, it is taught as an upper level movement in Classical dressage and as a Grand Prix level movement.

The half-pass is a movement where the horse is moving sideways and forward at the same time, while bent slightly in the direction of movement. The outside hind and forelegs should cross over the inside legs, with the horse's body parallel to the arena wall.

Collecting at the trot is a shortening of stride; the horse brings its hindquarters more underneath himself and carries more weight on his hind end. The tempo does not change, the horse simply shortens and elevates his stride.

Cantering the circle begins at the lowest levels and is later incorporated into the most difficult of Grand Prix tests.

"Pirouette" comes from the French, "to whirl about." As in all dressage, the horse should remain relaxed, engaged, and responsive, with the poll as the highest point.

At the lower levels of dressage, a bridle includes a plain cavesson, drop noseband, or flash noseband. At the upper levels a plain cavesson is used on a double bridle. Figure-eight (also called Grackle) nosebands are not allowed in pure dressage, however they are allowed in the dressage phase of eventing.

Walking on a loose rein is often the sign of a completed test and a reward many horses enjoy. The mount has done its job and will relax its topline as you exit the arena.

Although sometimes boisterous considering the formality of dressage, many competitions allow a victory gallop at the close of a level. Dressage horses love to stretch their legs as much as any others!

At the end of the day, a dressage horse is your beloved equine partner... no matter what it does to make you chuckle.

You often see professional grooms caring for people's horses between classes at recognized events. These are dedicated and skilled horse folk earning money toward their own equestrian pursuits.

"On the Bit" comic art, ©Ellen Sallas

Look for these coloring books in the Ellen Sallas series from Little Roni Publishers

- I LOVE RIDING LESSONS
- I LOVE CROSS-COUNTRY
- I LOVE DRESSAGE
- I LOVE TRAIL RIDING
- I LOVE PONIES
- I LOVE SHOW JUMPING
- I LOVE WESTERN RIDING
- COLOR ME SPLASHY
- I LOVE HUNTER / JUMPER
- EAT, SLEEP, HORSES
- BEEN THERE, DONE THAT (SPILLS)
- MY EQUINE VALENTINE
- HORSES BEING SILLY
- MY SILLY PONY TODDLER COLORING BOOK
- FLOWER POWER HORSES OF SPRING

Also from Ellen Sallas, 120 Pages of REAL art you color and hang! From Little Roni Publishers, 2015

REAL HORSE ART THAT YOU COLOR, FRAME, AND HANG!

A SPECIAL COLORING BOOK FOR HORSE LOVERS

About the Artist

Bestselling author and artist Ellen Sallas has been drawing horses even before she could walk. An avid horse lover herself, Ellen has been known to ride horses over hill and dale while daydreaming about stories yet written.

Ellen lives with her husband and vivid imagination in North Alabama.

Ellen and Amber competing at J3 in Mississippi

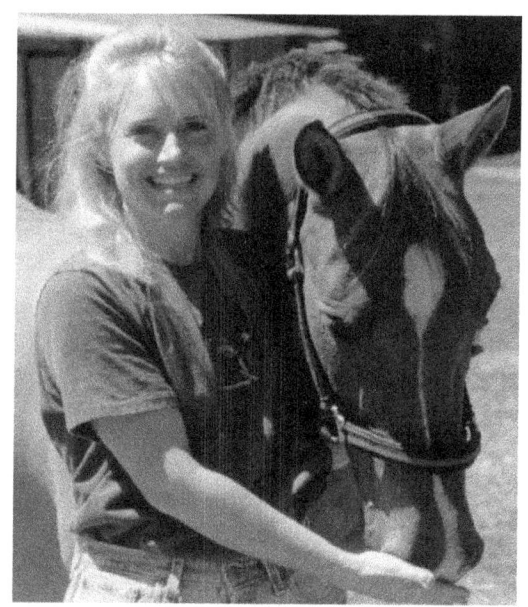

Ellen and Amber at Foxwood Farms Eventing Barn in Pike Road, AL

Ellen has sold her art worldwide as an acclaimed animal portraitist for nearly thirty years. You can purchase prints and originals at https://www.etsy.com/shop/giddyupstudio or by email, ellenmaze@aol.com.

Contact:

https://www.facebook.com/ellen.maze

https://twitter.com/ellenmaze

www.ellencmaze.com

www.LittleRoniPublishers.com